YOUR FAVORITE STARS

FEATURING
TAYLOR SWIFT

FACTS, QUIZZES, ACTIVITIES, AND MORE!

by Gena Chester

CAPSTONE PRESS
a capstone imprint

This is an unauthorized biography.

Published by Capstone Press, an imprint of Capstone
1710 Roe Crest Drive, North Mankato, Minnesota 56003
capstonepub.com

Copyright © 2026 by Capstone. All rights reserved. No part of this publication may be reproduced in whole or in part, or stored in a retrieval system, or transmitted in any form or by any means, electronic, mechanical, photocopying, recording, or otherwise, without written permission of the publisher.

Library of Congress Cataloging-in-Publication Data
Names: Chester, Gena, author.
Title: Featuring Taylor Swift : facts, quizzes, activities, and more! / Gena Chester.
Description: North Mankato : Capstone Press, 2025. | Series: Your favorite stars | Audience: Ages 8-11 | Audience: Grades 4-6 | Summary: "How many times does Taylor Swift mention the color red in her lyrics? How many times did Taylor change her outfit throughout an Eras tour concert? And what Easter eggs is she laying for her fans in her social media posts, videos, and more? Swifties can read all about this and more in this collection of fun facts, fabulous photos, and more, featuring the global superstar!"— Provided by publisher.
Identifiers: LCCN 2024055999 (print) | LCCN 2024056000 (ebook) | ISBN 9798875233258 (hardcover) | ISBN 9798875233203 (paperback) | ISBN 9798875233210 (pdf) | ISBN 9798875233227 (epub) | ISBN 9798875233234 (kindle edition)
Subjects: LCSH: Swift, Taylor, 1989- —Miscellanea—Juvenile literature. | Swift, Taylor, 1989- —Juvenile literature.
Classification: LCC ML3930.S989 L37 2025 (print) | LCC ML3930.S989 (ebook) | DDC 782.42164092 [B]—dc23/eng/20241122
LC record available at https://lccn.loc.gov/2024055999
LC ebook record available at https://lccn.loc.gov/2024056000

Editorial Credits
Editor: Julie Gassman; Designer: Elyse White; Media Researcher: Rebekah Hunstenberger; Production Specialist: Tori Abraham

Image Credits
Alamy: Taylor Swift Productions/Silent House/Album, 10, 39; Associated Press: Chris Pizzello/Invision, 4, 45, Chris Young/The Canadian Press, 40 (bottom); Getty Images: Arturo Holmes, 9 (bottom right), Christopher Polk, 28 (top), Ethan Miller, 8 (music video still), Frazer Harrison, 25, Gareth Cattermole, 20, 21, Jason Kempin, 27, JC Olivera, 14, 41 (middle), John Shearer, 6-7, Kevin Winter, 34, Kevork Djansezian, 7 (top), Kristy Sparow, 13, Lisa Maree Williams, 31 (top), 41 (top), Matt Winkelmeyer, 30 (Taylor Swift), 32 (Scooter Braun), 33, Michael Buckner, 5 (upper left), Mike Coppola, 35, Raymond Hall/GC Images, 23, Steph Chambers, 9 (top), Theo Wargo, 18; Newscom: ANTONI BYSZEWSKIFOTONEWS/ZUMAPRESS, 38, Mike Gray/Avalon, 43, TNS/Shanna Madison, front cover, VICTOR AUBRY/SIPA, 47; Shutterstock: 3d_kot, 24 (magnifiying glass), ABC vector, 11 (trees), Alexandr III, 32 (records), ANNA ZASIMOVA (rainbow chrome star), back cover and throughout, Chursina Viktoriia, 31 (nail polish), davorana, 10 (pocket watch), derter (rainbow chrome sparkle), back cover, 24, 41, Evgenia Vasileva, 26, Evgeniy245 (key), front cover, 2, 27, Fresh_Vector, 37 (vault), johavel, 5 (guitar), Kumeko, 45 (popcorn), Lightkite, 19 (film clapper), lilia_ahapova, 4 (heart), Luis Line (snake), front cover, 2, 29 (background), Mashaart (silver chrome star), back cover and throughout, MicroOne, 40 (friendship bracelet), missLEMON, 36 (leaves), MohammadKam, 16-17, 27 (heart hands), 30 (hearts), Net Vector, 13 (tear drop), quinky (butterfly), front cover, 2, 25, Ralph Biggör, 11 (disco ball), Rashad Ashur, 44 (broken heart), rzarek, 21 (flying paper), Shutterstock-Pixelsquid, 19 (gemstone), 28 (phone), Teodora ART, 21 (typewriter), Tuba Reza, 15, v_kulieva (blurry heart background), cover and throughout, vladwel, 8 (laptop)

Printed and bound in China. 6274

TABLE OF CONTENTS

CHAPTER 1: FEARLESS 4

CHAPTER 2: MASTERMIND 10

CHAPTER 3: "ACTION!" 18

CHAPTER 4: INVISIBLE STRINGS 24

CHAPTER 5: BEGIN AGAIN 32

CHAPTER 6: THE ERAS TOUR 38

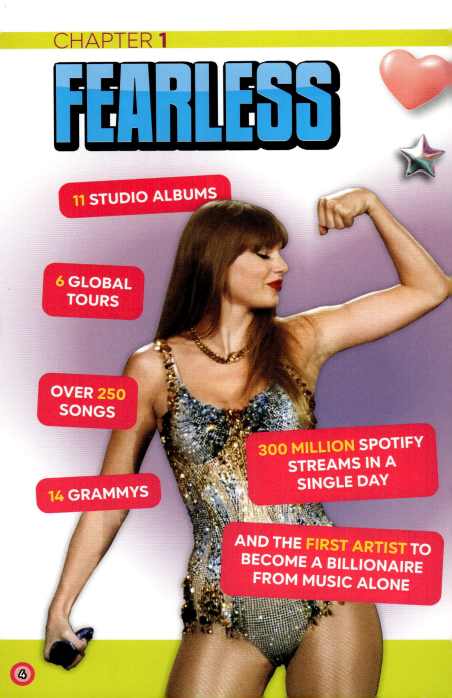

TAYLOR ALISON SWIFT has come a long way since growing up on a Christmas tree farm in Pennsylvania. The pop superstar has plenty of people behind her cheering her on. Her parents believed in her star power so much that they moved the family to Tennessee to pursue her dreams. The move kick-started countless eras and millions of lifelong fans.

HER SQUAD

Taylor has surrounded herself with many loyal people over her 20-year career. She's made plenty of friends that support her dream. During her 1989 era, she famously developed friendships with a special group of women, nicknamed her "squad." She's been a friend, bridesmaid, and even collaborated on music with members of her squad.

Taylor poses with friends Julien Baker, Lucy Dacus, and Phoebe Bridgers, who make up the band boygenius.

Taylor Swift's longtime music partner Jack Antonoff is also one of her besties. The duo have created more than 80 songs together.

STAR SCOOP!

Taylor's been best friends with Abigail Anderson Berard since high school. Taylor mentions Abigail in her hit song "**Fifteen**."

SQUAD AT WORK

For Taylor's iconic "**Bad Blood**" music video, she enlisted her squad to get into character. Here are some stars who made an appearance:

SELENA GOMEZ AS "ARSYN"

GIGI HADID AS "SLAY-Z"

ZENDAYA AS "CUT-THROAT"

KENDRICK LAMAR AS "WELVIN DA GREAT"

HAILEE STEINFELD AS "THE TRINITY"

Taylor attends Kansas City Chiefs games in style—and with friends! She's brought rapper Ice Spice, stylist Ashley Avignonoe, actress Blake Lively, and others to cheer on the NFL superstars.

STAR SCOOP!

During an Eras Tour concert, Taylor pulled out her phone and called bestie Sabrina Carpenter. Then the former Disney star joined Taylor onstage for a surprise mash-up of Carpenter's hits **"Espresso"** and **"Please Please Please"** with Taylor's **"Is It Over Now?"**

CHAPTER 2
MASTERMIND

Taylor is a **MASTERMIND**—and she knows it! She seamlessly blends moments from her life into beautiful lyrics. Much of her music is based on her real-life experiences. She references friends, romantic partners, and major life events! Taylor has said that writing helps her "get out the poison" and move on from difficult experiences.

STAR SCOOP!

While most of Taylor's albums are written about personal experiences, two are not. She has called *folklore* and *evermore* "imaginary." But still, many fans point to similarities between the albums' lyrics and Taylor Swift's life.

NAME THAT SONG

Guess which song goes with these popular lyrics!

1. "Cause the players gonna play, play, play, play, play . . ."

    A. "Shake It Off"
    B. "The Alchemy"
    C. "So High School"

2. "It's me, hi, I'm the problem, it's me . . ."

    A. "I Knew You Were Trouble"
    B. "Welcome to New York"
    C. "Anti-Hero"

3. "I love you, ain't that the worst thing you ever heard?"

    A. "Paper Rings"
    B. "Cruel Summer"
    C. "Love Story"

4. "She's cheer captain, and I'm on the bleachers . . ."

    A. "Our Song"
    B. "Fearless"
    C. "You Belong With Me"

5. "Cause, darling, I'm a nightmare dressed like a daydream . . ."

    A. "Blank Space"
    B. "Lavender Haze"
    C. "Fortnight"

STAR SCOOP!

Taylor wrote or cowrote all 31 songs on *The Tortured Poets Department.* Of those songs, most are rumored to be about exes Matty Healy and Joe Alwyn.

Answers: 1. A, 2. C, 3. B, 4. C, 5. A

WHO'S THIS SONG ABOUT ANYWAY?

- "DELICATE": JOE ALWYN
- "STYLE": HARRY STYLES
- "ALL TOO WELL": JAKE GYLLENHAAL
- "BAD BLOOD": KATY PERRY
- "THE BEST DAY": ANDREA SWIFT
- "SO HIGH SCHOOL": TRAVIS KELCE
- "I CAN DO IT WITH A BROKEN HEART": SWIFTIES

Travis Kelce

MAKE A LYRIC POSTER!

WHAT YOU NEED:
- Paper
- Writing utensil
- Art supplies

WHAT YOU DO:

1. Make a list of your favorite Taylor Swift songs. Listen through them and take note of your favorite lyrics.

2. Choose the song and lyrics you like best. Think about what the lyrics mean to you. How do you see those lyrics in your mind?

3. Use your art supplies to create a poster. Write out a favorite line and add pictures that go with the words. If you want to, add the song title. Your poster will be one of a kind!

REPEATING MAGIC

Taylor has an impressive music catalog under her belt, and with all of those songs, she's come back to certain themes and metaphors again and again. She's mentioned certain colors repeatedly throughout her songs.

RED: 72 TIMES

GOLD: 28 TIMES

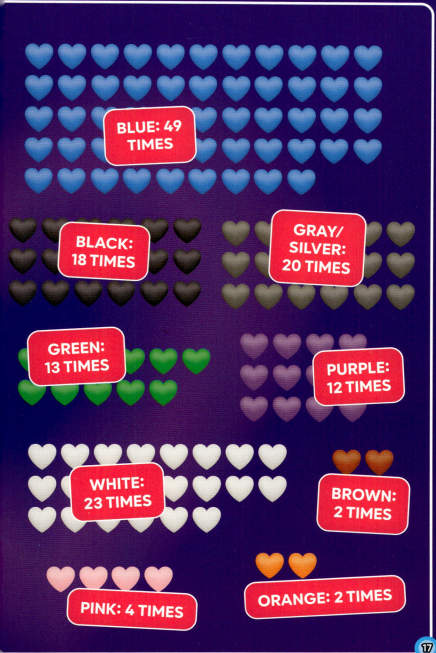

CHAPTER 3
"ACTION!"

In 2010, Taylor shot the music video for "**Mine**" from her *Speak Now* album. The shoot was a big step for Taylor, who was only 20 years old at the time. It was her first time shooting outside of Nashville, Tennessee. It was also her first taste of directing. Taylor wrote and co-directed the video with Roman White.

STAR SCOOP!

Taylor racked up awards for directing *All Too Well: The Short Film*, including Video of the Year at the MTV VMAs.

VIDEOS DIRECTED BY TAYLOR!

- "MINE" CO-DIRECTED WITH ROMAN WHITE
- "ME!" CO-DIRECTED WITH DAVE MEYERS
- "YOU NEED TO CALM DOWN" CO-DIRECTED WITH DREW KIRSCH
- "LOVER" CO-DIRECTED WITH DREW KIRSCH
- "CHRISTMAS TREE FARM"
- "THE MAN"
- "CARDIGAN"
- "WILLOW"
- "THE BEST DAY" (TAYLOR'S VERSION)
- "ALL TOO WELL: THE SHORT FILM"
- "ANTI-HERO"
- "BEJEWELLED"
- "LAVENDER HAZE"
- "KARMA"
- "I CAN SEE YOU"
- "FORTNIGHT"
- "I CAN DO IT WITH A BROKEN HEART"

ON HER OWN

Taylor's solo directorial debut happened by chance when she couldn't find a director for "**The Man**" music video in 2019. She also starred in the video, which follows a man in a series of scenes. Many viewers didn't realize it was her in disguise until the end credits!

Taylor described the experience of directing "The Man" as "more fulfilling than [she] could ever have imagined." She hasn't stopped since! She's gone on to direct more than 10 music videos by herself.

One of the outfits Taylor wore as "The Man" was part of a display of Taylor's costumes and outfits at a London museum during the summer of 2024.

STAR SCOOP!

Taylor wrote and directed the music video for "**Fortnight**." Her hard work paid off: the video was nominated for a Grammy!

CAT LADY

Taylor has a passion for life that expands past pop stardom. In addition to directing, she's branched out into acting and is a dedicated cat mom. She's adopted two Scottish folds named Olivia Benson and Meredith Grey. In 2019, she adopted Benjamin Button, a Ragdoll.

" . . . he looks at me like, 'You're my mom, and we're going to live together.' I fell in love." (About Benjamin)

"She's a scrappy little cat." (About Olivia)

"[Cats] are very dignified. They're independent. They're very capable of dealing with their own life."

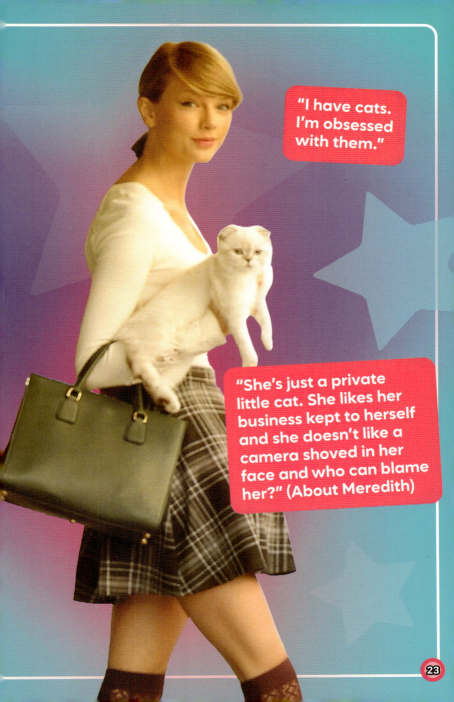

CHAPTER 4
INVISIBLE STRINGS

Taylor's not just a genius songwriter. She's also a master at leaving clues for her fans. Swifties live in excitement and fear for Taylor's every post—excitement because it gives them another glimpse into Taylor's mind, and fear because they don't want to miss any of their idol's Easter eggs.

Some of Taylor's Easter eggs come from her official fan account, Taylor Nation. Swifties consider posts from Taylor Nation as a message from Taylor herself.

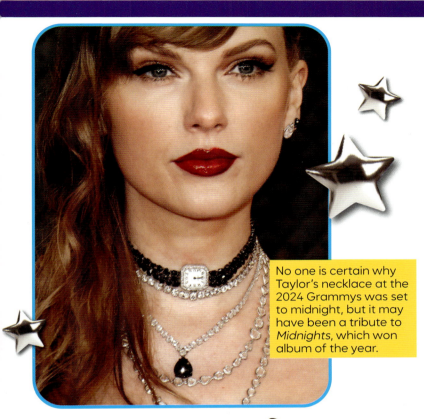

No one is certain why Taylor's necklace at the 2024 Grammys was set to midnight, but it may have been a tribute to *Midnights*, which won album of the year.

STAR SCOOP!

Taylor's clues have been present since her first album. Official lyrics included capital letters that spelled hidden messages. The message in "**Our Song**" is "live in love."

13 AND 1989!

Any post, caption, or story might be riddled with clues. Taylor's put Easter eggs in her music videos and pop-up art installations. Even her outfits are Easter eggs! Certain messages are often hidden over and over again throughout her work. For instance, Taylor is obsessed with the numbers **13** and **1989**, and it's one of her most-used Easter eggs. The numbers make up her birthdate: December 13, 1989.

STAR SCOOP!

Three days after Taylor announced her upcoming album, **The Tortured Poets Department**, Taylor Nation posted an Instagram with a caption starting with **"Fresh out the slammer** . . ." This was eventually revealed to be an Easter egg for a song title on **TTPD**.

1989

13

Taylor wrote 13 on her hand for good luck during her *Fearless* tour.

One of the inspirations behind "Look What You Made Me Do" is Kanye West, who interrupted Taylor's speech at the 2009 MTV Video Music Awards.

In Taylor's "**Look What You Made Me Do**" music video, a scene at the end showed Taylor with versions of her past selves. The visual went along with a line in the song: "The old Taylor is dead."

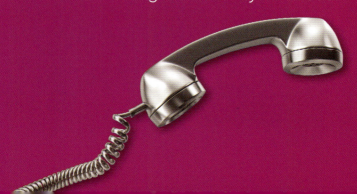

THE 14 LWYMMD TAYLORS:

- "YOU BELONG WITH ME" TAYLOR
- 2014 MET GALA TAYLOR
- *FEARLESS* MET GALA TAYLOR
- 2009 VMAS TAYLOR
- "SHAKE IT OFF" TAYLOR
- "WE ARE NEVER GETTING BACK TOGETHER" TAYLOR
- 2015 BILLBOARD AWARDS TAYLOR
- "22" TAYLOR
- ZOMBIE TAYLOR
- "BLANK SPACE" TAYLOR
- BASEBALL BAT TAYLOR
- THREE *REPUTATION* TAYLORS SHOWN EARLIER IN THE VIDEO

COLORS AS CLUES

Swifties love to discuss the colors Taylor wears and what they might mean. During one stop on her Eras Tour, Taylor switched all of her tour outfits to blue-toned versions. The color blue is often associated with her album *1989*. She finally announced her release of *1989 (Taylor's Version)* during her performance of "**New Romantics**"—a track on the album.

Fans remained hopeful that Taylor would have an all-green night to announce *Reputation (Taylor's Version)*. These hopes were dashed when the tour wrapped in December 2024 with no announcement.

A "TAYLORED" MANICURE!

Taylor had a multicolored manicure for the opening leg of her Eras Tour. Each nail represented one of her first 10 albums. Do your own Eras Tour manicure! Paint your nails in this order:

RIGHT HAND:

1. Thumb: black
2. Pointer: pink
3. Middle: gray
4. Ring: cream
5. Pinky: navy

LEFT HAND:

1. Thumb: turquoise
2. Pointer: red
3. Middle: plum
4. Ring: gold
5. Pinky: mint green

CHAPTER 5
BEGIN AGAIN

When Taylor Swift left her partnership with Big Machine Records, she wanted to buy the masters for her first six records. Instead, the record label sold them to talent manager Scooter Braun.

Scooter Braun

In a tweet, singer Kelly Clarkson suggested that Taylor re-record those records. The move would give Taylor ownership of all her music. Clarkson's advice launched a multiyear plan for Taylor to take her power back with a series of re-recordings. These versions are easy to spot: every new album and song has **"(TAYLOR'S VERSION)"** added after the original title.

STAR SCOOP!

Kelly Clarkson's tweet read: "@taylorswift13 just a thought, U should go in & re-record all the songs that U don't own the masters on exactly how U did them but put brand new art & some kind of incentive so fans will no longer buy the old versions. . . ."

A NEW ERA

While Taylor was working on re-recording her past albums, she also put out new music. The albums *folklore*, *evermore*, *Midnights*, and *The Tortured Poets Department* were added to her music catalog.

Taylor announced *TTPD* during her acceptance speech for the 2024 Grammy for Best Pop Vocal Album.

Taylor gave her fans one of her signature surprises with her *TTPD* release. She released a *double* album with a total of **31** tracks! The album was number one on the charts for 14 nonconsecutive weeks. Its first single, "**Fortnight**," broke the record for highest single-day streams on Spotify.

STAR SCOOP!

"**Fortnight**" features Post Malone. Taylor shared this about working with the singer and rapper: *". . . I'm so grateful to him for everything he put into this collaboration."* In return, Post Malone said: *"It's once in a lifetime that someone like @taylorswift13 comes into this world . . ."*

TAYLOR'S VAULT TRACKS

Taylor includes vault tracks on each of her re-recorded albums. These are songs that were originally written for, but never made it on, the original albums. Which are your favorites?

RED (TAYLOR'S VERSION)

"Better Man"
"Nothing New" (featuring Phoebe Bridgers)
"Babe"
"Message in a Bottle"
"I Bet You Think About Me" (featuring Chris Stapleton)
"Forever Winter"
"Run" (featuring Ed Sheeran)
"The Very First Night"
"All Too Well (10 Minute Version)"

FEARLESS (TAYLOR'S VERSION)

"You All Over Me" (featuring Maren Morris)
"Mr. Perfectly Fine"
"We Were Happy"
"That's When" (featuring Keith Urban)
"Don't You"
"Bye Bye Baby"

SPEAK NOW (TAYLOR'S VERSION)

"Foolish One"
"I Can See You"
"When Emma Falls in Love"
"Electric Touch" (featuring Fall Out Boy)
"Timeless"
"Castles Crumbling" (featuring Hayley Williams)

1989 (TAYLOR'S VERSION)

"Say Don't Go"
"Now That We Don't Talk"
"Is It Over Now?"
"Suburban Legends"

CHAPTER **6**

THE ERAS TOUR

STAR SCOOP!

The Eras Tour set list was over three hours long and included more than 40 songs, with an additional two surprise songs that varied at every concert. The Eras Tour was perfectly named—the songs cover albums from her entire career.

When Taylor announced she would be touring in 2023, fans were more than ready to see their idol onstage. The popstar hadn't been on the road since her Reputation Stadium Tour in 2018. Taylor had planned a Lover Fest tour in 2020, but unfortunately it was canceled due to the COVID-19 pandemic. The hype for her Eras Tour was off the charts. When ticket sales opened, the Ticketmaster website crashed!

SO MAKE THE FRIENDSHIP BRACELETS

Most of the fans who went to an Eras Tour concert dressed in their favorite era and exchanged dozens of friendship bracelets. The bracelets are a nod to a line in her song "You're On Your Own, Kid." Taylor talked about the bracelets at one tour stop in New Orleans. She said, **"You've created this mass movement of joy every time we play a show, and it makes me so proud. . . ."**

Huge friendship bracelets appeared at the last four stops on the tour. They were shared from city to city.

STAR SCOOP!

Travis Kelce tried to give Taylor a friendship bracelet when he attended the Eras Tour but wasn't able to connect. He told the story of his missed opportunity on his podcast, and Taylor reached out to meet with him soon after.

GUESS THE ERA OUTFIT!

1. Which era featured sparkly gold or silver dresses with fringe that moved as Taylor danced?

- A. Fearless
- B. Speak Now
- C. Midnights

2. Which era had Taylor in a T-shirt and black hat?

- A. Lover
- B. TTPD
- C. Red

3. Which era starts with Taylor in a white dress with writing on the skirt?

- A. Reputation
- B. TTPD
- C. 1989

4. Which era put Taylor in a one-legged bodysuit?

    A. Reputation
    B. Lover
    C. Evermore

5. Which era features a sparkly pair of boots paired with a sparkly blazer?

    A. Fearless
    B. Speak Now
    C. Lover

STAR SCOOP!

Throughout each concert, Taylor changed outfits about 16 times. She had multiple outfits to choose from for every era. Fans loved to guess which outfits would appear for each concert.

Answers: 1. A, 2. C, 3. B, 4. A, 5. C

THE BIG SCREEN

TAYLOR SWIFT: THE ERAS TOUR premiered in theaters in October 2023. It featured a recording of one of Taylor's Los Angeles shows. For many fans, this was the only way to experience her tour. Moviegoers stood up and sang along as Taylor performed onscreen.

Fans didn't have to worry if they missed the movie in theaters. The music film was released on Disney+ in March 2024. In the first three days of its release, fans had streamed it **4.6 MILLION** times.

STAR SCOOP!

Taylor changed her set list midtour. She cut some songs to make room for *TTPD*, complete with new outfits and choreography. One song she added, **"I Can Do It with a Broken Heart,"** was about performing on the Eras Tour.

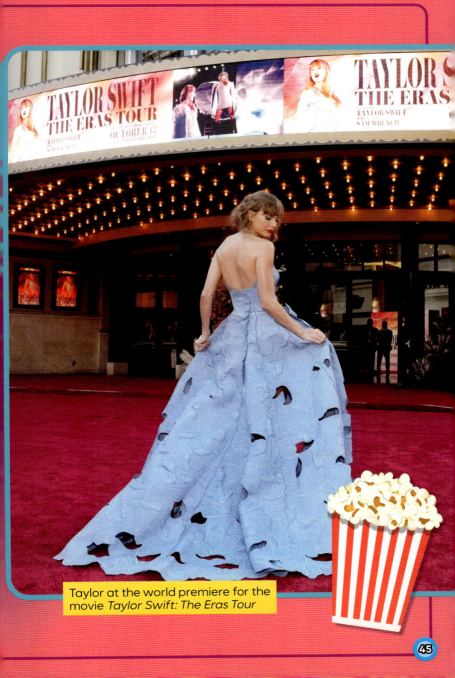
Taylor at the world premiere for the movie *Taylor Swift: The Eras Tour*

ERAS TOUR
BY THE NUMBERS

With a tour as big as Eras, it's bound to bring in some impressive figures. No matter how you calculate it, the numbers behind the Eras Tour are staggering. During Eras, Swift became the first artist to become a billionaire through music alone.

6.02 MILLION (ESTIMATED) TICKETS SOLD

60+ ONSTAGE OUTFITS

145 DIFFERENT SONGS PLAYED (COUNTING HER SURPRISE SONGS)

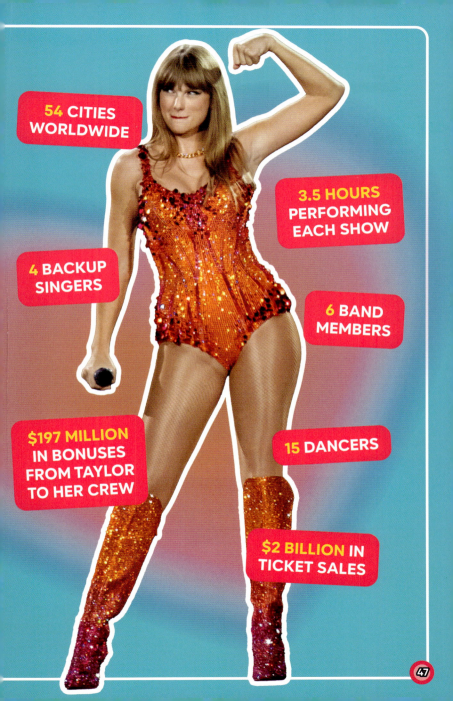

ABOUT THE AUTHOR

Gena Chester has been a dedicated Swiftie since the first time she listened to "Our Song" in 2006. She's followed every album release and incorporated Taylor's songs into every party she has ever thrown. The greatest moment of her life, aside from giving birth to her son, was attending the Eras Tour in Minneapolis, Minnesota. She is on a mission to convert friends and family into fellow Swifties and will stop at nothing until everyone becomes a fan!

READ MORE ABOUT YOUR FAVORITE STARS